What Is Math?

Tracey Steffora

www.heinemannraintree.com
Visit our website to find out
more information about
Heinemann-Raintree books.

To order:

☎ Phone 888-454-2279

▣ Visit www.heinemannraintree.com
to browse our catalog and order online.

© 2012 Heinemann Library
an imprint of Capstone Global Library, LLC
Chicago, Illinois

Customer Service: 888-454-2279
Visit our website at www.heinemannraintree.com

Edited by Rebecca Rissman, Daniel Nunn, and Harriet Milles
Designed by Joanna Hinton-Malivoire
Picture research by Elizabeth Alexander
Originated by Capstone Global Library Ltd.
Production by Victoria Fitzgerald
Printed and bound in China by Leo Paper Products Ltd

15 14 13 12 11
10 9 8 7 6 5 4 3 2 1

Library of Congress Cataloging-in-Publication Data
Steffora, Tracey.
   What is math? / Tracey Steffora.
      p. cm.
   Includes bibliographical references and indexes.
   ISBN 978-1-4329-5356-0 (hc)—ISBN 978-1-4329-5501-4 (pb) 1.
Mathematics—Juvenile literature. I. Title.
   QA39.2.S68985 2012
   510—dc22   2010044800

Acknowledgments
The author and publishers are grateful to the following for
permission to reproduce copyright material: Alamy **p. 7** (©
STOCKFOLIO®); © Capstone Publishers **pp. 14, 15, 18** (Karon
Dubke); Getty Images **pp. 12** (Tooga/The Image Bank), **13**
(Andersen Ross/Stockbyte); iStockphoto **pp. 5, 22 top left**
(© Stacey Newman), **10, 22 bottom right** (© Lauri Wiberg);
Photolibrary **p. 17** (Richard Hutchings); Shutterstock **pp. 4** (©
Alexander Chaikin), **8** (© Nick Stubbs), **9** (© Alfred Krzemien),
11 (© Sophie Bengtsson), **16** (© auremar), **19, 22 top right** (©
pixshots), **20** (© Stephen Coburn), **21, 22 bottom left** (© PeterG).

Front cover photograph of a) colored pencils reproduced with
permission of Shutterstock (© djem), and b) simple math witih
permission of iStockphoto (© Hande Guleryuz Yuce). Back cover
photograph of a young girl counting red apples reproduced with
permission iStockphoto (© Stacey Newman).

We would like to thank Patricia Wooster for her invaluable help in
the preparation of this book.

Every effort has been made to contact copyright holders of any
material reproduced in this book. Any omissions will be rectified in
subsequent printings if notice is given to the publisher.

Some words appear in bold, **like this**. You can find out
what they mean in "Words to Know" on page 23.

Contents

About this series

Books in this series introduce readers to simple math concepts through child-friendly contexts. Use this book to stimulate discussion about what math is and how it is part of daily life.

What Is Math?

There is math in everything we do. There is math in everything we see. How many yellow vans can you see in the picture?

Math is a way we understand the world. Math is all around us.

Math Is Shapes

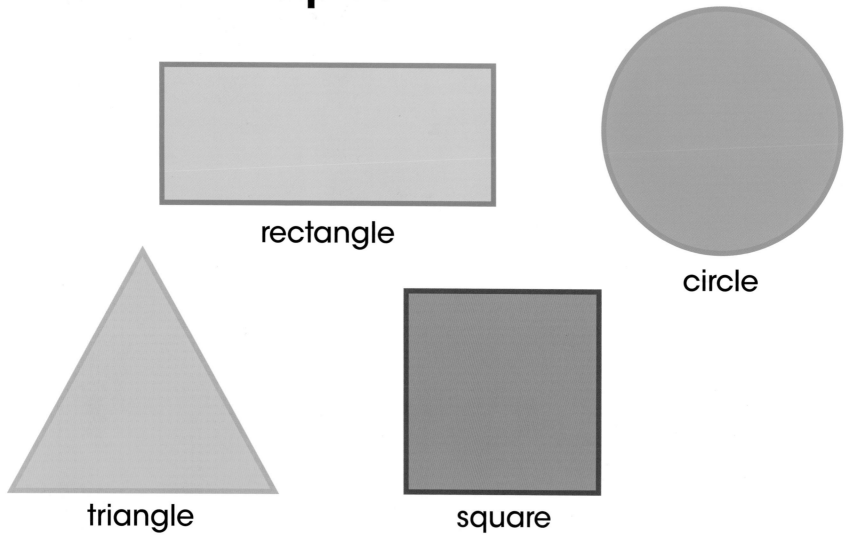

rectangle

circle

triangle

square

Everything has a **shape**. Some shapes have special names. Squares, rectangles, triangles, and circles are examples of shapes that have special names.

side

corner

Shapes can have sides and corners. Shapes can be big and small. You can see shapes everywhere you go. What shapes can you see in this picture?

Math Is Patterns

Sometimes things have a special order to them. This order is called a **pattern**. A pattern can be things in a row that get larger or smaller. A pattern can be things that **repeat**.

Numbers can be a pattern. **Shapes** can be a pattern. Colors can be a pattern. There are patterns everywhere you look.

Math Is Sorting

When you **sort** things, you put them into groups. We sort to help us organize and find things.

There are many things we can sort. We can sort things by color. We can sort things by size. We can sort things by **shape**. We can sort things by how they are used.

Math Is Counting

Sometimes it is important to know how many there are of something. We **count** things to find out how many there are.

Numbers help us count. We can count many things. Counting happens all around us.

Math Is Adding

When we **count** more of something, we are **adding**.
This person is adding eggs to a pancake batter.

Math Is Subtracting

Subtracting means taking something away. When we subtract something, we have fewer things left. If we take one cupcake away, how many will be left?

Math Is Measuring

scales

Do you ever want to know how much there is of something? Do you ever want to know how tall or how heavy something is? Sometimes we use **scales** to help us **measure** how heavy things are.

thermometer

Do you ever want to know how hot or cold something is? Measuring can give you the answer. A **thermometer** can measure how hot or cold it is outside.

ruler

Sometimes we use special tools to measure.
This girl is using a tool called a **ruler** to measure
some flowers!

Sometimes we measure by **comparing**. We compare things to see if something is bigger or smaller.

People Using Math

People use math at school and at work. This man is **measuring** the wood he needs to build a house.

People use math at home. This cook is measuring oil to put into food.

Index

Note to Parents and Teachers

Before reading

Show the children the front cover of the book. Ask them if they can see anything around them that shows math. Explain to the children that math is all around us through shapes, numbers, counting, and in many other ways.

After reading

- Fill a plastic bag with different types of colored shapes, and give each child one bag. Ask them, "Are there different ways to sort these shapes?" Some possible answers may be: by size, shape, and color. Ask the children to pick one way to sort their shapes, and explain to a partner why they sorted the shapes in the way they did. After they have sorted the shapes, introduce some addition and subtraction exercises. For example, they could add up squares plus triangles, or red shapes plus blue shapes.